MW01537687

This Notebook Belongs To
